JUST BRASS

directed by

Philip Jones and Elgar Howarth

FRANCIS POULENC
SONATA

for Horn, Trumpet and Trombone
(1922)

parts included for:

1 Horn in F
2 Trumpet in C
3 Trombone

Duration: 8 minutes

This work has been recorded by the
Philip Jones Brass Ensemble
on
Argo ZRG 731

CHESTER MUSIC LIMITED

(A division of Music Sales Limited)

SONATA

for Horn, Trumpet and Trombone

(1922)

Score in C

I. Allegro Moderato

Francis Poulenc

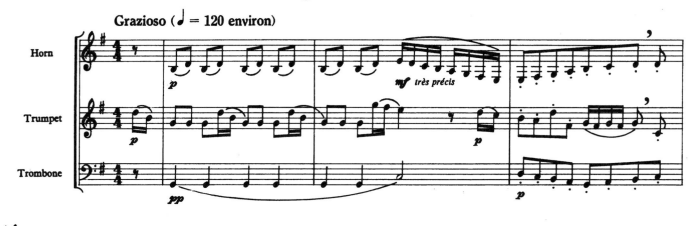

CH55111

Cédez peu à peu

20

Plus lent (♪ = 104)

30

Solo

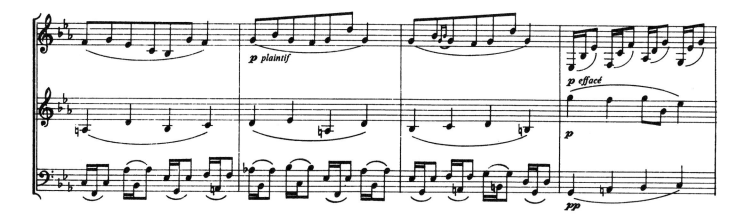

Pressez peu à peu

40
Subitement vite sans presser (♩ = 144)

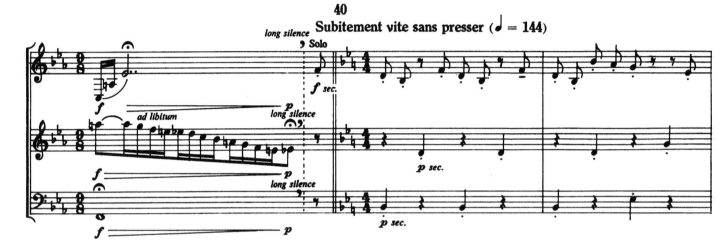

50

Cédez un peu

Tempo I⁰ (♩ = 120)   **60**

(♩ = 126)

SONATA

for Horn, Trumpet and Trombone

(1922)

2 Trumpet in C

Francis Poulenc

I. Allegro Moderato

CH55111c

III. Rondeau

2 Trumpet in C

SONATA

for Horn, Trumpet and Trombone

(1922)

1 Horn in F

Francis Poulenc

I. Allegro Moderato

1 Horn in F

III. Rondeau

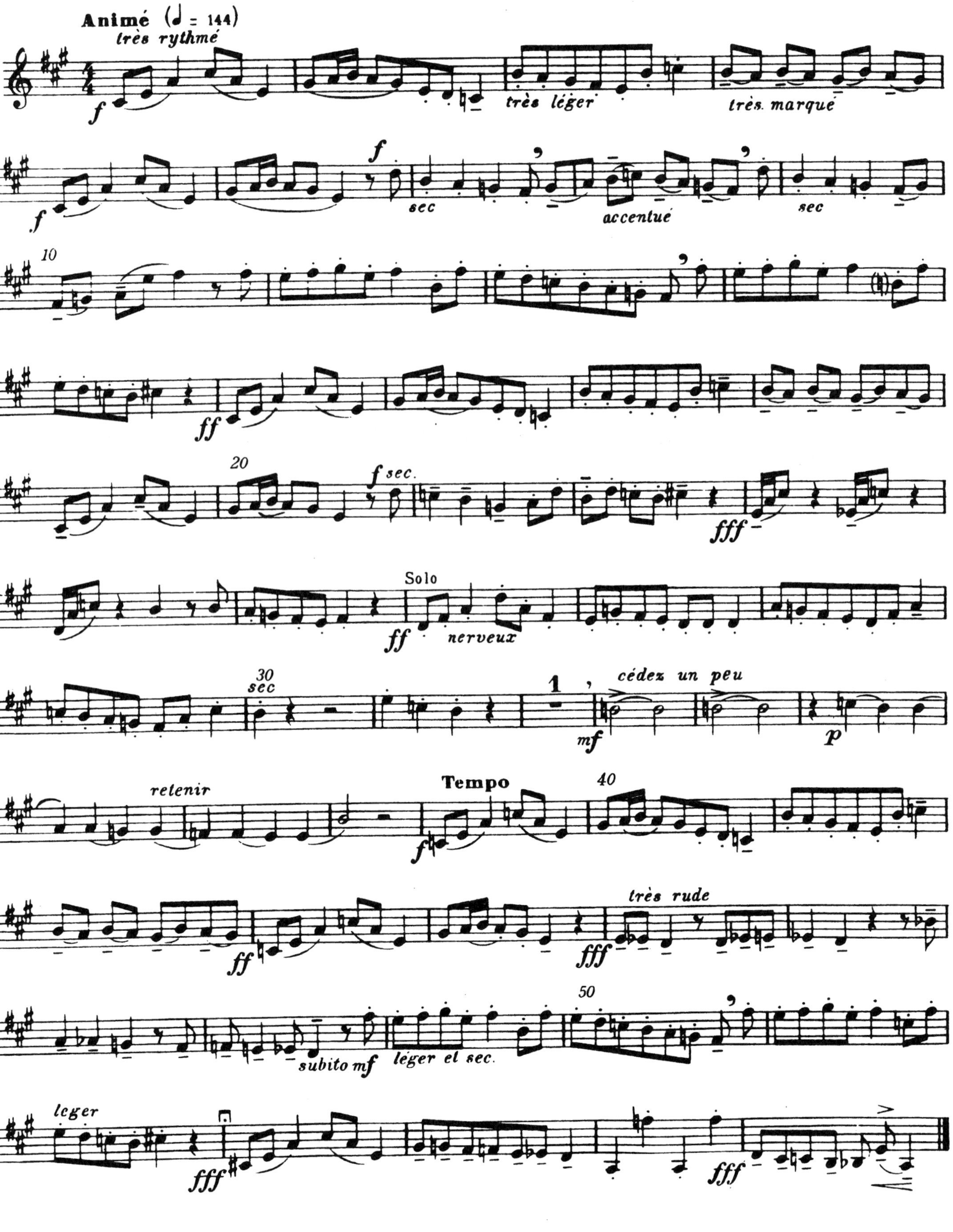

SONATA

for Horn, Trumpet and Trombone

(1922)

2 Trumpet in B♭

Francis Poulenc

I. Allegro Moderato

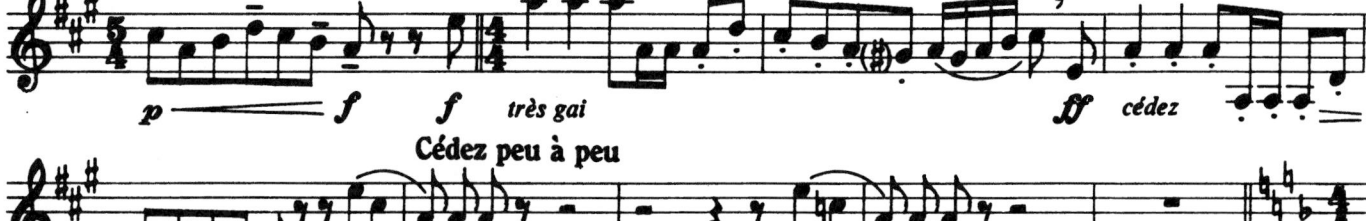

2 Trumpet in B♭

III. Rondeau

Cédez peu à peu

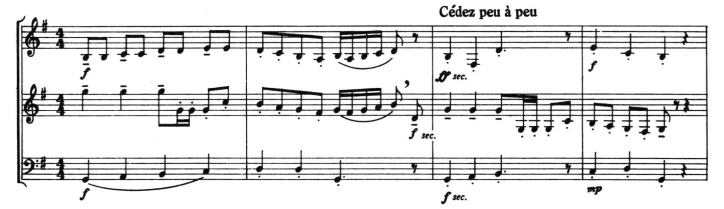

Lent

II. Andante

Très lent (♪ = 76)

Horn

Trumpet

Trombone

10

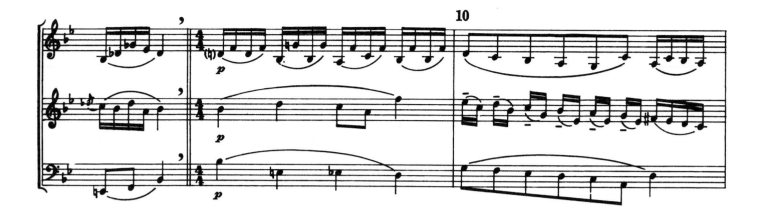

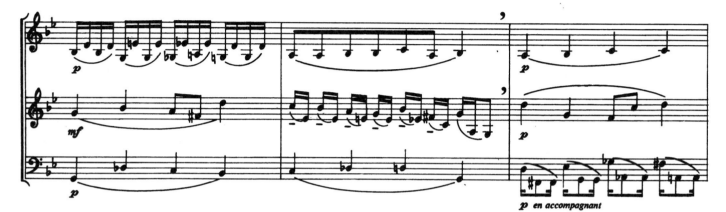

Solo

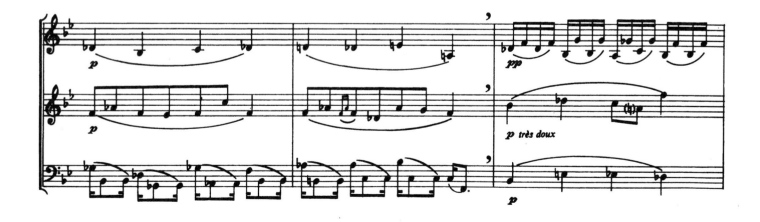

20

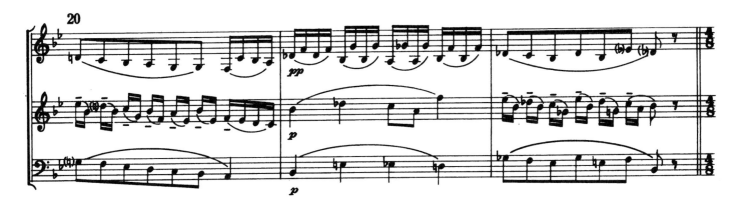

III. Rondeau

Animé (♩ = 144)

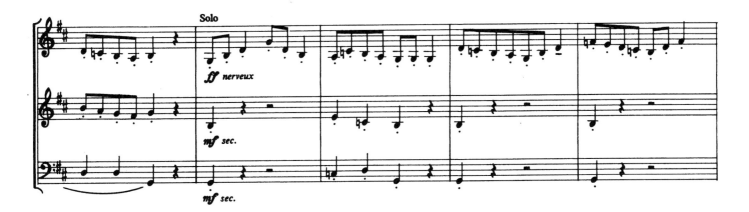

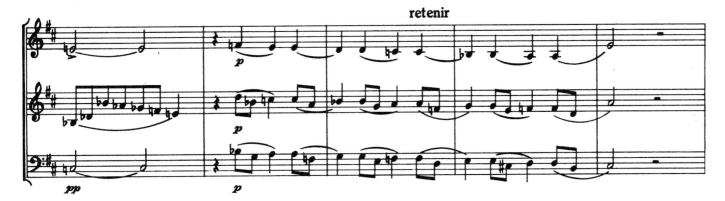

50